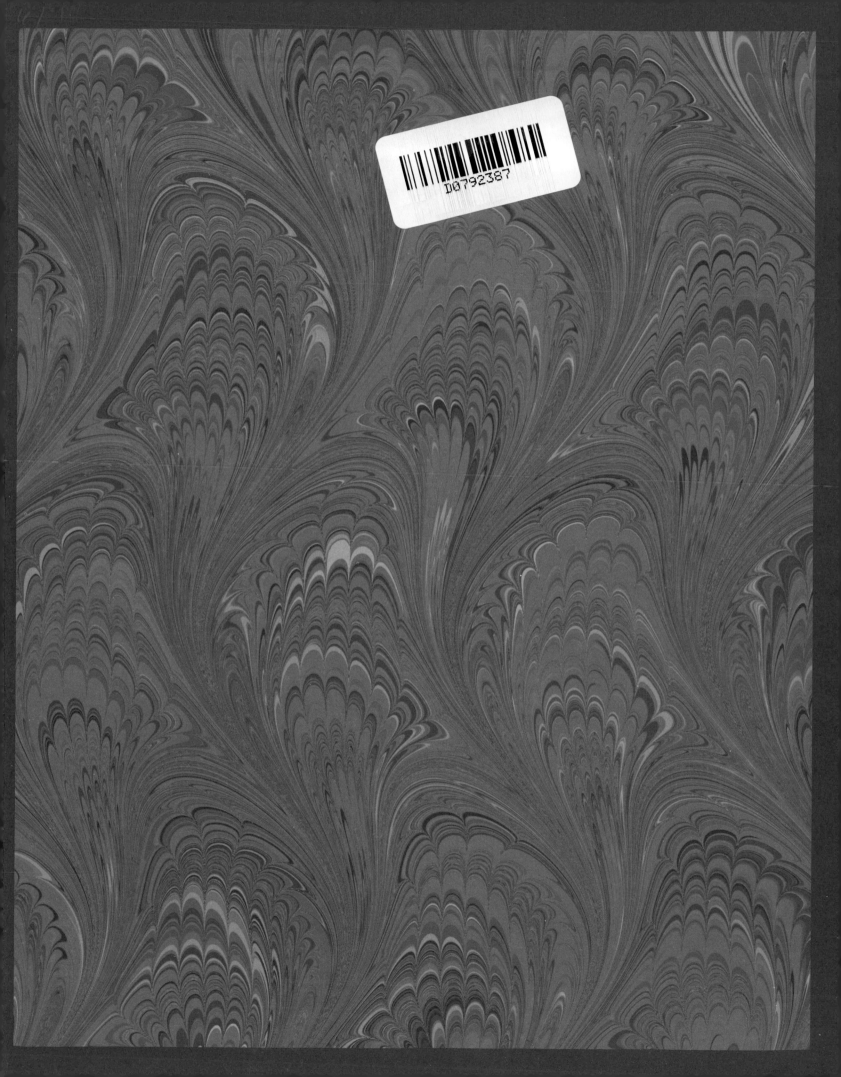

METAMORPHOSIS

ALSO BY MIKE WILKS

Pile - Petals From St Klaed's Computer
The Weather Works
The Ultimate Alphabet
The Annotated Ultimate Alphabet
The BBC Drawing Course
The Ultimate Noah's Ark

FOR CHILDREN
In Granny's Garden

ALSO BY MIKE WILKS

Pile - Petals From St. Klaeds Computer
The Weather Works
The Ultimate Alphabet
The Annotated Ultimate Alphabet
The BBC Drawing Course
The Ultimate Noah's Ark.

FOR CHILDREN
In Granny's Garden

METAMORPHOSIS

THE ULTIMATE
SPOT-THE-DIFFERENCE
BOOK

MIKE WILKS

METAMORPHOSIS

THE ULTIMATE
SPOT-THE-DIFFERENCE
BOOK

MIKE WILKS

PENGUIN
STUDIO

INTRODUCTION

What will have immediately struck you, even at a casual glance, is that this book is strange. It is unlike any book you have seen before. Each facing page has been printed twice. This was not done to waste paper. Neither was it done to make the book appear fatter than it would otherwise have been. Look again at these words on the opposite page. They are not quite identical to the ones on this. The same is true of all the other pages. Intrigued? Then read on.

This is the starting point for a visual adventure that begins with a paradox: *the only unchanging thing in the universe is change itself*. Everything else, including the universe, is transitory.

The lifetime of the universe is, by definition, for ever. When the universe ends so will time. So will space. But other things dance to a quicker tune than the stately gavotte of the cosmos.

On our own small planet continents slither about on the surface of the world like infinitely ponderous skaters on tectonic skates. This all happens between heartbeats on the grand time scale of the universe.

Dancing to the quickstep of history, civilisations rise and fall, gods and religions come and go and nation states blink in and out of existence. Everything is in motion, everything is temporary. Only change never changes.

Change is happening all the time. Looked at one way, change *is* time. Looked at another, it is space. Looked at yet another way - the way I prefer - change is simply change. Everyone recognises it for what it is.

The pages of this book are changing even as you read these words but, viewed from our mortal perspective, so imperceptibly slowly that you will not notice. A short while ago they were trees. In a few years time (quite a few, I hope)

INTRODUCTION

hat will have immediately struck you, even at a casual glance, is that this book is strange. It is unlike any book you have seen before. Each facing page has been printed twiice. This was not done to waste paper. Neither was it done to make the book appear fatter than it would otherwise have been. Look again at these words on the opposite page. They are not quite identical to the ones on this. The same is true of all the other pages. Intrigued? Then read on.

This is the starting point for a visual adventure that begins with a paradox; *the only unchanging thing in the universe is change itself*. Everything else, including the universe, is transitory.

The lifetime of the universe is, by definition, for ever. When the universe ends so will time. So will space. But other things dance to a quicker tune than the stately gavote of the cosmos.

On our own small planet continents slither about on the surface of the world like infinitely ponderous skaters on tectonic skates. This all happens between heart-beats on the grand time scale of the universe.

Dancing to the quickstep of history, civilisations rise and fall, gods and religions come and go and nation states blink in and out of existence. Everything is in motion, everything is temporary. Only change never changes.

Change is happening all the time. Looked at one way, change *is* time. Looked at another, it is space. Looked at yet another way - the way 1 prefer - change is simply change. Everyone recognizes it for what it is.

The pages of this book are changing even as you read these words but, viewed from our mortal perspective, so imperceptibly slowly that you will not notice. A short while ago they were trees. In a few years time (quite a few, I hope) they will be recycled into something else. With luck they might have an afterlife as something useful like lavatory paper or loft insulation. Without it they might take several steps backwards down the karmic scale and end up wrapping small tubes of carcinogenic vegetable matter, sold in packs of twenty. They might simply decay into some kind of amorphous gunge. Whatever happens, whenever it happens, they are going to change.

Some changes are abrupt but most are relatively slow. Looked at this way there are no solid objects, only events. Mostly brief ones at that.

Except on an intellectual level, changes on such a cosmic time scale as those taking place in the universe mean little to you and me. We sometimes talk about 'seeing history being made' when witnessing some important occasion but this is merely a figure of speech. Generally we encounter only the consequences of history.

The empirical changes that we all witness are those from day to night, the turning of the seasons, watching our children grow up and our parents grow old. The biggest change that we will have first-hand experience of is that of a lifetime. A frantic jitterbug - almost a blur - even when compared to something dancing as fast as history. The paintings reproduced in this book depict this great, yet brief, human cycle.

This series starts with birth (which I do not remember) in *Nativity* and ends with death (which I can only anticipate) in *The Glowing Assassins Take Pride in Their Work*. Between these two inevitable bookends that both confine and define our lives are my personal responses to some of the milestones that we all have to pass. Although these images are highly personal and depict my own inner vision, I am sure that you will also recognise similar stages in your own life and in the lives of those around you.

Lucifer's Garden concerns infancy. In it I tried to capture something of that magical time before memory became a conscious thing. A time when we were in this world but not yet quite of it.

The Septic Academy symbolises the time I spent at school. I remember this as a traumatic and humiliating period of my life. At the time I thought that it would last for ever. I memorised a great many things there but learnt nothing.

After school came art school and I learnt to dance *The Acorn Dance*. There I memorised nothing and learnt every-

they will be recycled into something else. With luck they might have an afterlife as something useful like lavatory paper or loft insulation. Without it they might take several steps backwards down the karmic scale and end up wrapping small tubes of carcinogenic vegetable matter, sold in packs of twenty. They might simply decay into some kind of amorphous gunge. Whatever happens, whenever it happens, they are going to change.

Some changes are abrupt but most are relatively slow. Looked at this way there are no solid objects, only events. Mostly brief ones at that.

Except on an intellectual level, changes on such a cosmic time-scale as those taking place in the universe mean little to you and me. We sometimes talk about "seeing history being made" when witnessing some important occasion but this is meerly a figure of speech. Generally we encounter only the consequences of history.

The empirical changes that we all witness are those from day to night, the turning of the seasons, watching our children grow up and our parents grow old. The biggest change that we will have first-hand experience of is that of a lifetime. A frantic jitterbug - almost a blur - even when compared to something dancing as fast as history. The paintings reproduced in this book depict this great, yet brief, human cycle.

This series starts with birth (which I do not remember) in *Nativity* and ends with death (which I can only anticipate) in *The Glowing Assassins Take Pride in Their Work*. Between these two inevitable bookends that both confine and define our lives are my personal responses to some of the milestones that we all have to pass. Although these images are highly personal and depict my own inner vision, I am sure that you will also recognise similar stages in your own life and in the lifes of those around you.

Lucifers' Garden concerns infancy. In it I tried to capture something of that magical time before memory became a conscious thing. A time when we were in this world but not yet quite of it.

The Septic Academy symbolises the time I spent at school. I remember this as a traumatic and humiliating period of my life. At the time I thought that it would last for ever. I memorized a great many things there but learnt nothing.

After school came art school and I learnt to dance *The Acorn Dance*. There I memorised nothing and learnt every-

thing that I have since found useful in life.

Brides and Blizzards Have White in Common concerns the search for a partner. Although I have chosen to place it here, where most people experience this part of their lives, for me it is a search that continues.

My studio is the geographical centre of my life. Physically surrounding that is my home. *The House of Second Thoughts* depicts this subject.

Sooner or later we must all accept responsibility. From that point on a part of our lives is spent in *The Gravity Mine*.

If my physical home is represented in the image mentioned before then *The Invention of Faraway Places* symbolises my emotional home which is my work. Here is where I spend the major part of my life. It is the perspective from which I view everything else.

The View from La Roque concerns the acceptance of one's own dual nature, the unique mix of good and bad that makes us what we are.

Achievement, in both the professional and personal sense of the word, is represented in *The Cannibal Luncheon Club*. Some eat lunch, some *are* lunch.

Light Sleeper concerns retrospection. One day we awaken to find that the view to the past is clearer than that to the future.

To complement these images I have chosen excerpts from great works of world literature on the theme of transformation. These and the other chosen extracts reflect my eclectic nature and my interest in anything strange or unorthodox. Included is the oldest known written work from Ancient Egypt, created more than 4,000 years before the most recent one. In that cosmic blink of an eye, art changed very little.

Likewise, my paintings are not so very different from those painted on the walls of caves about 20,000 years ago. The prehistoric artist and I both manipulated coloured molecules on a flat surface. But after my panels were complete I made the changes to the images with a computer and exchanged pigment for pixels, my brushes for an electronic stylus and gesso panels for silicon chips. Art changes at its own speed, but it changes nevertheless.

This visual adventure chronicling a journey through life is also a puzzle on the grand theme of change in the same way as life itself is a puzzle on that selfsame theme. You will have already noticed some of the differences, the inconstant echoes, in this book. There are more. Lots more. Just how many there are is for you to tell me. Look at the double pages in this book. On each left-hand page is an image or a piece of

 thing that I have since found useful in life.

Brides and Blizzard's Have White in Common concerns the search for a partner. Although I have chosen to place it here, where most people experience this part of their lives, for me it is a search that continues.

My studio is the geographical center of my life. Physically surrounding that is my home. *The House of Second Thoughts* depicts this subject.

Sooner or later we must all accept responsibility. From that point on a part of our lives is spent in *The Gravity Mine*.

If my physical home is represented in the image mentioned before then *The Invention of Faraway Places* symbolizes my emotional home which is my work. Here is where I spend the major part of my life. It is the perspective from which I view everything else.

The View from La Rogue concerns the acceptance of ones' own dual nature, the unique mix of good and bad that makes us what we are.

Achievement, in both the professional and personal sense of the word, is represented in *The Cannibal Luncheon Club*. Some eat lunch, some *are* lunch.

Light Sleeper concerns retrospection. One day we awaken to find that the view to the past is clearer than that to the future.

To compliment these images I have chosen excerpts from great works of world literature on the theme of transformation. These and the other chosen extracts reflect my eclectic nature and my interest in anything strange or unorthodox. Included is the oldest known written work from Ancient Egypt, created more than 4,000 years before the most recent one. In that cosmic blink of an eye, art changed very little.

Likewise, my paintings are not so very different from those painted on the walls of caves about 20,000 years ago. The prehistoric artist and I both manipulated coloured molecules on a flat surface. But after my panels were complete I made the changes to the images with a computer and exchanged pigment for pixels, my brushes for an electronic stylus and gesso panels for silicon chips. Art changes at its own speed, but it changes nevertheless.

This visual adventure chronicling a journey through life is also a puzzle on the grand theme of change in the same way as life itself is a puzzle on that selfsame theme. You will have already noticed some of the differences, the inconstant echoes, in this book. There are more, Lots more. Just how many there are is for you to tell me. Look at the double pages in this book. On each left-hand page is an image or a piece of text that is not quite identical to the one facing it. To find these differences all you will need is patience and a pair of eyes. Even one eye will do. Nothing else is necessary. You will not need to consult voluminous encyclopaedias or fat dictionaries or haunt the great libraries of the world in order to fathom these changes. Everything you need you have with you at this instant.

A change is a change but you will find there are various flavours of change. You will see that I have made major changes, which you will spot right away, and minor changes, which are subtle and might elude you for a while. I have blown some things up and shrunk other things down. Here and there I have changed the orientation of things from right to left or from left to right (and even from top to bottom). To some elements I have added things, while to others I have removed them. Some objects will have changed their position and others their colour. On pages with images there are never more than 250 changes and on those with words never more than 75. There is at least one difference between every double page.

Here are two details from one of the pictures. There are 23 differences between them. Indulge in some visual callisthenics and see if you can find them.

When I was creating this book I had quite a few changes of pace, countless changes of mood and plenty of changes of mind. But none of these is apparent in the final work and only the physical ones need to be counted.

To keep track of the differences you discover, you can mark them on the page if you are the kind of scoundrel who enjoys inflicting notes on a defenceless book. If you are not, then you might make notes on a sheet of tracing paper placed over each page. What I did, as I was perpetrating the changes, was to circle each one on a photocopy as I proceeded. This worked fine for me but you might come up with an even better way. Just because you have found one difference between two items, do not move on

text that is not quite identical to the one facing it. To find these differences all you will need is patience and a pair of eyes. Even one eye will do. Nothing else is necessary. You will not need to consult voluminous encyclopædias or fat dictionaries or haunt the great libraries of the world in order to fathom these changes. Everything you need you have with you at this instant.

A change is a change but you will find there are various flavours of change. You will see that I have made major changes, which you will spot right away, and minor changes, which are subtle and might elude you for a while. I have blown some things up and shrunk other things down. Here and there I have changed the orientation of things from right to left or from left to right (and even from top to bottom). To some elements I have addedd things, while to others I have remove them. Some objects will have changed their position and others their colour. On pages with images there are never more than 250 changes and on those with words never more than 75. There is at least one difference between every double page.

Here are two details from one of the pictures. There are 33 differences between them. Indulge in some visual callisthenics and see if you can find them.

When I was creating this book I had quite a few changes of pace, countless changes of mood and plenty of changes of mind. But none of these is apparent in the final work and only the physical ones need to be counted.

To keep track of the differences you discover, you can mark them on the page if you are the kind of scoundrel who enjoys inflicting notes on a defenseless book. If you are not, then you might make notes on a sheet of tracing paper placed over each page. What I did, as I was perpetrating the changes, was to circle each one on a photocopy as I proceeded. This worked fine for me but you might come up with an even better way. Just because you have found one difference between two items, do not move on immediately. There might be another concealed within that same object. The position might have changed as well as the colour. And the text may not give up all its secrets at first glance either. Look at the context as well as the appearance. You may be surprised at what you find.

There are two questions about my work that I can guarantee I will be asked: 'How long does it take you?' and, 'Where do you get your ideas from?' By the first, people invariably mean 'How long did it take you to squeeze the paint from its tube, whack it down and push it around until it looked like it does?' No account is taken of the years at art school or the years spent afterwards when I struggled to make the paint look like anything other than paint. Left to its own devices it has a pronounced tendency to look like itself. Paint is innately lazy stuff. To this question I can normally come up with a response that satisfies the preconceptions of my interrogator.

The second question is rather more difficult to answer. For me, ideas fall into just two categories – bad and good. Into the first category must fall such ideas as processed cheese, the Spanish Inquisition, cigarettes and cannibalism. In the second you might find painless dentistry, electric lighting, the wines of Château Margaux and the entire works of Johann Sebastian Bach.

Where ideas come from is a mystery. Could they be conceptual viruses that infect those among us already weakened by a tenuous grasp on reality (whatever *that* might mean)? Perhaps they are for ever drifting around in the æther and become attracted to receptive minds by a kind of osmosis. Or else they may be like invisible time-bombs silently ticking away to detonate at a certain predetermined instant in time, splatter-ing any bystander in their vicinity with conceptual shrapnel. Maybe the bad ideas are those that explode prematurely or inefficiently or too far away. Who knows?

But the *real* trouble with ideas is not where they come from. It is that once you have had one it cannot be un-had. Victor Hugo said: 'A stand can be made against invasion by an army; no stand can be made against invasion by an idea.' Bad or good they just will not go away. They must come out. That's when problems really begin.

I know well the sensation when an idea has detonated near me. There is that old familiar feeling of elation mixed with foreboding that I am letting myself in for yet another heap of trouble. It will be necessary to cancel all appointments for the next few years. Then there will be materials to purchase, brush-es and colours to replace and research material to order. When this is all satisfactorily in place, a kind of long, dogged slog will begin, to be punctuated at regular intervals by insomnia, indiges-tion, muscular cramps, black despair and manic euphoria. Another

immediately. There might be another concealed within that same object. The position might have changed as well as the colour. And the text may not give up all its secrets at first glance either. Look at the context as well as the appearance. You may be surprized at what you find.

There are two questions about my work that I can guarantee I will be asked; 'How long does it take you?' and, 'Where do you get your ideas from?' By the first, people invariably mean 'How long did it take you to squeeze the paint from its tube whack it down and push it around until it looked like it does?' No account is taken of the years at art school or the years spent afterwards when I struggled to make the paint look like anything other than paint. Left to its own devices it has a pronounced tendency to look like itself. Paint is innately lazy stuff. To this question I can normally come up with a response that satisfies the preconceptions of my interrogator.

The second question is rather more difficult to answer. For me, ideas fall into just two categories – bad and good. Into the first category must fall such ideas as processed cheese, the Spanish inquisition, cigarettes and cannibalism. In the second you might find painless dentistry, electric lighting, the wines of Chateau Margaux and the entire works of Johann Sebastian Bach.

Where ideas come from is a mystery. Could they be conceptual viruses that infect those among us already weakened by a tenuous grasp on reality (whatever *that* might mean?) Perhaps they are for ever drifting around in the œther and become attracted to receptive minds by a kind of osmosis. Or else they may be like invisible time bombs silently ticking away to detonate at a certain predetermined instant in time, spattering any bystander in their vicinity with conceptual shrapnel. Maybe the bad ideas are those that explode prematurely or inefficiently or too far away. Who knows?

But the *real* trouble with ideas is not where they come from. It is that once you have had one it cannot be un–had. Victor Hugo said; 'A stand can be made against invasion by an army: no stand can be made against invasion by an idea." Bad or good they just will not go away. They must come out. Thats when problems really begin.

I know well the sensation when an idea has detonated near me. There is that old familiar feeling of elation mixed with foreboding that I am letting myself in for yet another heap of trouble. It will be necessary to cancel all appointments for the next few years. Then there will be materials to purchase, brushes and colours to replace and research material to order. When this is all satisfactorily in place, a kind of long, dogged slog will begin, to be punctuated at regular intervals by insomnia, indigestion, muscular cramps, black despair and manic euphoria. Another new project is under way.

This book began its life in the predictable way. The serious injuries that I sustained from the original exploding idea developed complications. Secondary, then tertiary, infections set in which were subsequently diagnosed as an obsession. In my occasional lucid moments I thought to record the progress of all this. The results as this obsession advanced and suppurated from my mind on to the panels, are reproduced here in all their gory and clinical detail as a warning to others.

There is only one way to treat this kind of a problem and my malady necessitated a strict régime. Rise at first light and begin working right away. A short break at midday for light refreshment and continue working until the light has failed. This prescription to be taken seven days a week for as long as it takes. In the case of this book 'as long as it took' meant four years of actual painting - that is, squeezing paint from tubes, whacking it down and pushing it around until it looked like it does.

Often, when I risked losing control of an idea, I found it necessary to backtrack and rework a portion of the panel. Whenever I am faced with the prospect of making a compromise in my work, I forcefully remind myself that it is likely to be around for much longer than I ever will. I may never live long enough to use a piece of lavatory paper recycled from one of my books.

Then there comes a point when most people imagine that a painting is 'finished'. In truth what happens is that it becomes progressively less rewarding to continue working and the image is eventually abandoned. All of the paintings in this book were abandoned after three, four or, in one case, nine months work. I then had the images scanned into a computer and spent more time manipulating the resulting coloured pixels into the changes evident in their not quite mirror images.

Afterwards there was more time spent researching and compiling the text, and then the editing and checking of all the proofs and the time involved in a variety of activities that helped bring the idea to the attention of the book-buying public. But, when all is said and done, the only true cure for an obsession is to replace it with another - something I have since done.

That was my part in this project. Your part is to use your eyes, those highly sensitive, stereoscopic, light receptors that constitute an outgrowth of the forebrain. These are outwardly protected by lashes

new project is under way.

This book began its life in the predictable way. The serious injuries that I sustained from the original exploding idea developed complications. Secondary, then tertiary, infections set in which were subsequently diagnosed as an obsession. In my occasional lucid moments I thought to record the progress of all this. The results as this obsession advanced and suppurated from my mind on to the panels, are reproduced here in all their gory and clinical detail as a warning to others.

There is only one way to treat this kind of a problem and my malady necessitated a strict règime. Rise at first light and begin working right away. A short break at mid-day for light refreshment and continue working until the light has failed. This prescription to be taken seven days a week for as long as it takes. In the case of this book 'as long as it took' meant four years of actual painting - that is, squeezing paint from tubes, whacking it down and pushing it around until it looked like it does.

Often, when I risked losing control of an idea, I found it necessary to backtrack and rework a portion of the panel. Whenever I am faced with the prospect of making a compromise in my work, I forcefully remind myself that it is likely to be around for much longer than I ever will. I may never live long enough to use a piece of lavatory paper recycled from one of my books.

Then there comes a point when most people imagine that a painting is 'finished', In truth what happens is that it becomes progressively less rewarding to continue working and the image is eventually abandoned. All of the paintings in this book were abandoned after three, four or, in one case, nine months work. I then had the images scanned into a computer and spent more time manipulating the resulting coloured pixels into the changes evident in their not quite mirror images.

Afterwards there was more time spent researching and compiling the text, and then the editing and checking of all the proofs and the time involved in a variety of activities that helped bring the idea to the attention of the book-buying public. But, when all is said and done, the only true cure for an obsession is to replace it with another - something I have since done.

That was my part in this project. Your part is to use your eyes, those highly sensitive, stereoscopic, light recepters that constitute an outgrowth of the forebrain. These are outwardly protected by lashes and lids that also periodically moisten the eyes by a momentary reflexive closing, which briefly coats the eyeball with lubricating fluid. Six extraocular muscles attached to each eyeball can move them up and down and from side to side. Visual energy in the form of light travelling at 2.997925×10^8 metres per second (approximately 300,000 kilometres or 186,000 miles per second) is reflected indiscriminately off objects as diverse as walruses' whiskers, plates of *magret de canard*, pin-up calendars, rainbows, the Empire State Building and the words you are reading here.

The light then passes through the cornea to the lens via the iris from where it travels on to the retina at the back of the eye. There it is detected by light receptors (rod cells) and colour receptors (cone cells), which contain pigment molecules. When the light stimulates these molecules they trigger a chemical transmitter that initiates an electrical message that is passed by the optic nerve to the brain (if present). Between five and ten photons are sufficient to trigger a response in one of our 240 million rods but it takes 250 photons to stimulate one of our 12 million cones.

Five to ten photons is the amount of light emitted by a candle when seen from a distance of about 16 kilometres (roughly ten miles or the distance travelled by a single-minded garden snail in 45.89 days if it does not pause to eat or sleep).

Your eyes are capable of discerning about nine million separate colours that are combinations of the three primary colours of light - red, blue and green. These colours have wavelengths of between about 400 and 700 nanometres (billionths of a metre). This is known as the visible spectrum and never quite seems to contain the particular colour I am searching for. This signal is received upside down in opposite cerebral hemispheres where it is inverted to appear normal (whatever *that* might mean).

So, as you look at these rectangles of compressed wooden particles covered with paint stains made from irregularly-shaped splodges of coloured pigment suspended in emulsified acrylic polymer reproduced in the pages of this book with those wondrous, sensitive, self-regulating, colour-receiving, stereoscopic peepers - of all the photons that stimulated the molecules and then transmitted the electro-chemical messages to the cells in your brain, just how many differences can you spot?

and lids that also periodically moisten the eyes by a momentary reflexive closing, which briefly coats the eyeball with lubricating fluid. Six extraocular muscles attached to each eyeball can move them up and down and from side to side. Visual energy in the form of light travelling at 2.997925×10^8 metres per second (approximately 300,000 kilometres or 186,000 miles per second(is reflected indiscriminately off objects as diverse as walruses' whiskers, plates of *magret de canard*, pin-up calendars, rainbows, the Empire State Building and the words you are reading here.

The light then passes through the cornea to the lens via the iris from where it travels on to the retina at the back of the eye. There it is detected by light receptors (rod cells) and colour receptors (conn cells), which contain pigment molecules. When the light stimulates these molecules they trigger a chemical transmitter that initiates an electrical message that is passed by the optic nerve to the brain (if present). Between five and ten photons are sufficient to trigger a response in one of our 240 million rods but it takes 280 photons to stimulate one of our 12 million cones.

Five to ten photons is the amount of light emitted by a candle when seen from a distance of about 16 kilometres (roughly ten miles or the distance travelled by a single-minded garden snail in 45,86 days if it does not pause to eat or sleep).

Your eyes are capable of discerning about nine million separate colours that are combinations of the three primary colours of light - red, blue and green. These colours have wavelengths of between about 400 and 700 nanametres (billionths of a metre). This is known as the visible spectrum and never quite seems to contain the particular colour I am searching for. This signal is received upside down in opposite cerebral hemispheres where it is inverted to appear normal (whatever *that* might mean).

So, as you look at these rectangles of compressed wooden particles covered with paint stains made from irregularly-shaped spludges of coloured pigment suspended in emulsified acrylic polymer reproduced in the pages of this book with those wondrous, sensitive, self-regulating, colour-receiving, stereoscopic peepers - of all the photons that stimulated the molycules and then transmitted the electro-chemical messages to the cells in your brain, just how many differences can you spot?

An Ant nimbly running about in the sunshine in search of food came across a Chrysalis that was very near its time of change. The Chrysalis moved its tail, and thus attracted the attention of the Ant, who then saw for the first time that it was alive. 'Poor, pitiable animal!' cried the Ant disdainfully. 'What a sad fate is yours! While I can run hither and thither, at my pleasure, and, if I wish, ascend the tallest tree, you lie imprisoned here in your shell, with power only to move a joint or two of your scaly tail.' The Chrysalis heard all this, but did not try to make any reply. A few days after, when the Ant passed that way again, nothing but the shell remained. Wondering what had become of its contents, he felt himself suddenly shaded and fanned by the gorgeous wings of a beautiful Butterfly. 'Behold in me,' said the Butterfly, 'your much-pitied friend! Boast now of your powers to run and climb as long as you can get me to listen.' So saying, the Butterfly rose in the air, and, borne along and aloft on the summer breeze, was soon lost to the sight of the Ant forever.

Appearances are deceptive.

From *Aesop's Fables – The Ant and the Chrysalis* by Aesop

An Ant nimbly running about in the sunshine in search of food came across a Chrysalis that was very near its time of change. The Chrysalis moved its tail, and thus attracted the attention of the Ant, who then saw for the first time that it was alive. 'Poor, pitiable animal!" cried the Ant disdainfully. 'What a sad fate is yours! While I can run thither and hither, at my pleasure, and, if I wish, ascend the tallest tree, you lie imprisoned here in your shell, with power only to move a joint or two of your scaly tail.' The Chrysalis heard all this, but did not try to make any reply. A few days after, when the Ant passed that way again, nothing but the shell remained. Wondering what had become of its contents, he felt himself suddenly shaded and fanned by the gorgeous wings of a beautiful Butterfly. 'Behold in me,' said the butterfly, 'your much pitied friend! Boast now of your powers to run and climb as long as you can get me to listen.' So saying, the Butterfly rose in the air, and, borne along and aloft on the summer breeze, was soon lost to the sight of the Ant for ever.

Appearances are deceptive

From *Aesops Fables - The Ant & the Chrysalis* by Aesop

NATIVITY

NATIVITA

'hat a curious feeling!' said Alice. 'I must be shutting up like a telescope!'

And so it was indeed: she was now only ten inches high, and her face brightened up at the thought that she was now the right size for going through the little door into that lovely garden. First, however, she waited for a few minutes to see if she was going to shrink any further: she felt a little nervous about this; 'for it might end, you know,' said Alice to herself, 'in my going out altogether, like a candle. I wonder what I should be like then?' And she tried to fancy what the flame of a candle looks like after the candle is blown out, for she could not remember ever having seen such a thing.

After a while, finding that nothing more happened, she decided on going into the garden at once; but, alas for poor Alice! when she got to the door, she found she had forgotten the little golden key, and when she went back to the table for it, she found she could not possibly reach it: she could see it quite plainly through the glass and she tried her best to climb up one of the legs of the table, but it was too slippery; and when she had tired herself out with trying, the poor little thing sat down and cried.

'Come, there's no use in crying like that!' said Alice to herself, rather sharply. 'I advise you to leave off this minute!' She generally gave herself very good advice (though she seldom followed it), and sometimes she scolded herself so severely as to bring tears into her eyes; and once she remembered trying to box her own ears for having cheated herself in a game of croquet she was playing against herself, for this curious child was very fond of pretending to be two people. 'But it's no use now,' thought poor Alice, 'to pretend to be two people! Why there's hardly enough of me left to make one respectable person!'

Soon her eye fell on a little glass box that was lying under the table: she opened it, and found in it a very small cake, on which the words 'EAT ME' were beautifully marked in currants. 'Well, I'll eat it,' said Alice, 'and if it makes me grow larger, I can reach the key; and if it makes me grow smaller, I can creep under the door: so either way I'll get into the garden, and I don't care which happens!'

She ate a little bit, and said anxiously to herself, 'Which way? which way?', holding her hand on the top of her head to feel which way it was growing; and she was quite surprised to find that she remained the same size. To be sure, this is what generally happens when one eats cake; but Alice had got so much into the way of expecting nothing but out-of-the-way things to happen, that it seemed quite dull and stupid for life to go on in the common way.

So she set to work, and very soon finished off the cake.

From *Alice's Adventures in Wonderland* by Lewis Carroll

hat a curious feeling!' said Alice. 'I must be shutting up like a telescope!'

And so it was indeed; she was now only ten inches high, and her face brightened up at the thought that she was now the right size for going through the little door into that lovely garden. First, however, she waited for a few minutes to see if she was going to shrink any further: she felt a little nervous about this; 'for it might end, you know,' said Alice to herself, 'in my going out altogether, like a candle. I wonder what I should be like then?' And she tried to fancy what the flame of a candle looks like after the candle is blown out, for she could not remember ever having seen such a thing.

After a while, finding that nothing more happened, she decided on going into the garden at once; but, alss for poor Alice! when she got to the door, she found she had forgotten the little golden key, and when she went back to the table for it, she found she could not possibly reach it: she could see it quite plainly through the glass and she tried her best to climb up one of the legs of the table, but it was too slippery; and when she had tired herself out with trying, the poor little thing sat down and cried.

'Come, there's no use in crying like that!' said Alice to herself, rather sharply. 'I advise you to leave off this minute!' She generally gave herself very good advice (though she seldom followed it}, and sometimes she scolded herself so severely as to bring tears into her eyes: and once she remembered trying to box her own ears for having cheated herself in a game of croquet she was playing against herself, for this curious child was very fond of pretending to be two people. 'But it's no use now,' thought poor Alice, 'to pretend to be too people! Why, there is hardly enough of me left to make one respectable person!'

Soon her eye fell on a little glass box that was lying under the table: she opened it, and found in it a very small cake, on which the words 'EAT ME' were beautifully marked in currents. 'Well, I'll eat it,' said Alice, "and if it makes me grow larger, I can reach the keys; and if it makes me grow smalller, I can creep under the door: so either way I'll get into the garden, and I don't care which happens!'

She ate a little bit, and said anxiously to herself, 'Which way? which way?', holding her hand on the top of her head to feel which way it was growing; and she was quite surprised to find that she remained the same size, To be sure, this is what generally happens when one eats cake; but Alice had got so much into the way of expecting nothing but out-of the-way things to happen, that it seemed quite dull and stupid for life to go on in the common way.

So she set to work and very soon finished off the cake.

From *Alice's Adventures in Wonderland* by Lewis Carrol

LUCIFER'S GARDEN

LUCIFERS GARDEN

It was on a dreary night of November that I beheld the accomplishment of my toils. With an anxiety that almost amounted to agony, I collected the instruments of life around me, that I might infuse a spark of being into the lifeless thing that lay at my feet. It was already one in the morning; the rain pattered dismally against the panes, and my candle was nearly burnt out, when, by the glimmer of the half-extinguished light, I saw the dull yellow eye of the creature open; it breathed hard, and a convulsive motion agitated its limbs.

How can I describe my emotions at this catastrophe, or how delineate the wretch whom with such infinite pains and care I had endeavoured to form? His limbs were in proportion, and I had selected his features as beautiful. Beautiful! - Great God! His yellow skin scarcely covered the work of muscles and arteries beneath; his hair was of a lustrous black, and flowing; his teeth of a pearly whiteness; but these luxuriances only formed a more horrid contrast with his watery eyes, that seemed almost of the same colour as the dun white sockets in which they were set, his shrivelled complexion and straight black lips.

The different accidents of life are not so changeable as the feelings of human nature. I had worked hard for nearly two years, for the sole purpose of infusing life into an inanimate body. For this I had deprived myself of rest and health. I had desired it with an ardour that far exceeded moderation; but now that I had finished, the beauty of the dream vanished, and breathless horror and disgust filled my heart. Unable to endure the aspect of the being I had created, I rushed out of the room, and continued a long time traversing my bedchamber, unable to compose my mind to sleep. At length lassitude succeeded to the tumult I had before endured; and I threw myself on the bed in my clothes, endeavouring to seek a few moments of forgetfulness. But it was in vain: I slept, indeed, but I was disturbed by the wildest dreams.

From *Frankenstein or, The Modern Prometheus* by Mary Wollstonecraft Shelley

It was on a dreary night of November that I beheld the accomplishment of my toils. With an anxiety that almost amounted to agony, I collected the instruments of life around me, that I might infuse a spark of being into the lifeless thing that lay at my feet. It was already one in the morning; the rain pattered dismally against the panes, and my candle was nearly burnt out, when, by the glimmer of the half–extinguished light, I saw the dull yellow eye of the creature open; it breathed hard, and a convulsive motion agitated it's limbs.

How can I describe my emotions at this catastrophe, or how delineate the wretch whom with such infinite pains and care I had endeavoured to form? His limbs were in proportion, and l had selected his features as beautiful. Beautiful! - Great God! His yellow skin scarcely covered the work of muscles and arteries beneath; his hair was of a lustrous black, and flowing; his teeth of a pearly whiteness: but these luxuriances only formed a more horrid contrast with his watery eyes, that seemed almost of the same colour as the dun white sockets in which they were set, his shrivelled complexion and straight black lips.

The different accidents of life are not so changeable as the feelings of human nature. I had worked hard for nearly two years, for the sole purpose of infusing life into an insnimate body. Łor this I had deprived myself of rest and health. I had desired it with an ardor that far exceeded moderation; but now that I had finished, the beauty of the dream vanished, and breathless horror and disgust filled my heart. Unable to endure the aspect of the being I had created, I rushed out of the room, and continued a long time traversing my bed-chamber, unable to compose my mind to sleep. At length lassitude succeeded to the tumult I had before endured; and I threw myself on the bed in my clothes, endeavouring to seek a few moments of forgetfulness. But it was in vain: I slept, indeed, but I was disturbed by the wildest dreams.

From *Frankenstein or, The Modern Prometheus* by Mary Wollstoncraft Shelley

'**ir,**' said I, affecting a coolness that I was far from truly possessing, 'you speak enigmas, and you will perhaps not wonder that I hear you with no very strong impression of belief. But I have gone too far in the way of inexplicable services to pause before I see the end.'

'It is well,' replied my visitor. 'Lanyon, you remember your vows: what follows is under the seal of our profession. And now, you who have so long been bound to the most narrow and material views, you who have denied the virtue of transcendental medicine, you who have denied your superiors - behold!'

He put the glass to his lips and drank at one gulp. A cry followed; he reeled, staggered, clutched at the table and held on, staring with injected eyes, gasping with open mouth; and as I looked there came, I thought, a change - he seemed to swell - his face became suddenly black and the features seemed to melt and alter - and the next moment, I had sprung to my feet and leaped back against the wall, my arm raised to shield me from that prodigy, my mind submerged in terror.

'O God!' I screamed, and 'O God!' again and again; for there before my eyes - pale and shaken, and half fainting, and groping before him with his hands, like a man restored from death - there stood Henry Jekyll!

From *The Strange Case of Dr Jekyll and Mr Hyde* by Robert Louis Stevenson

ir,' said I, affecting a coolness that I was far from truly possessing, 'you speak enigmas, and you will perhaps not wonder that I hear you with no very strong impression of belief. But I have gone too far in the way of inexplicable services to pause before I see the end.'

'It is well,' replied my visitor. 'Lanyon, you remember your vows: what follows is under the seal of our proffession. And now, you who have so long been bound to the most narrow and material views, you who have denied the virtue of transcendental medicine, you who have denied your superiors - behold!'

He put the glass to his lip and drank at one gulp. A cry followed: he reeled, staggered, clutched at the table and held on, staring with injected eyes, gasping with open mouth; and as I looked there came, I thought, a change - he seemed to swell - his face became suddenly black and the features seemed to melt and alter - and the next moment, I had sprung to my feet and leaped back against the wall, my arm raised to shield me from that prodigy, my mind submerged in terror.

'O God!' I screamed, and, 'O God!' again and again; for there before my eyes - pale and shaken, and half fainting, and groping before him with his hands, like a man restored from death - there stood Henry Jekyll!

From *The Strange Case of Dr Jekll and Mr Hyde* by Robert Louis Stevenso

THE ACORN DANCE

THE ACORN DANCE

here, in an instant, I beheld uprisen
At once three hellish furies, stain'd with blood:
In limb and motion feminine they seem'd;
Around them greenest hydras twisting roll'd
Their volumes; adders and cerastes crept
Instead of hair, and their fierce temples bound.
He, knowing well the miserable hags
Who tend the queen of endless woe, thus spake:
'Mark thou each dire Erynnis. To the left,
This is Megæra; on the right hand, she
Who wails, Alecto; and Tisiphone
I' th' midst.' This said, in silence he remain'd.
Their breast they each one clawing tore; themselves
Smote with their palms, and such thrill clamour raised.
That to the bard I clung, suspicion-bound.
'Hasten Medusa: so to adamant
Him shall we change;' all looking down exclaim'd:
'E'en when by Theseus' might assail'd we took
No ill revenge.' 'Turn thyself round, and keep
Thy countenance hid; for if the Gorgon dire
Be shown, and thou shouldst view it, thy return
Upwards would be for ever lost. This said,
Himself, my gentle master, turn'd me round;
Nor trusted he my hands, but with his own
He also hid me. Ye of intellect
Sound and entire, mark well the lore conceal'd
Under close texture of the mystic strain.

From *The Divine Comedy* by Dante

There, in an instant, I behold uprisen
At once three hellish furies, stained with blood:
In limb and motion feminine they seem'd;
Around them greenest hydras twisting roll'd
Their volumes; adders and cerastes crept
Instead of hair, and their fierce temples bound.
He, knowing well the miserable hags'
Who tend the Queen of endless woe, thus spake:
'Mark thou each dire Erynnis. To the left,
This is Megaera; on the right hand, she
Who wails, Alecto; and Tisiphone
I' th' midst.' This said, in silence he remain'd.
Their breast they each one clawing tore: themselves
Smote with their palms, and such thrill clamour rais'd.
That to the Bard I clung, suspicion bound.
'Hasten Medusa: so to adamant
Him shall we change;, all looking down exclaim'd:
'E'en when by Theseus' might assail'd we took
No ill revenge.' 'Turn thyself round, and keep
Thy countenance hid; for if the gorgon dire
Be shown, and thou shouldst view it, thy return
Upwards would be for ever lost. This said,
Himself, my gentle master, turned me round;
Nor trusted he my hands, but with his own
He also hid me. Ye of intellect
Sound and entire, mark well the lore congeal'd
Under close texture of the mystic strain.

From *The Divine Comedy* by Danté

BRIDES & BLIZZARDS HAVE WHITE IN COMMON

BRIDES & BLIZZARDS HAVE WHITE IN COMMON

Bacchus, on a certain occasion, found his old schoolmaster and foster-father, Silenus, missing. The old man had been drinking, and in that state wandered away, and was found by some peasants, who carried him to their king, Midas. Midas recognised him, and treated him hospitably, entertaining him for ten days and nights with an unceasing round of jollity. On the eleventh day he brought Silenus back, and restored him in safety to his pupil. Whereupon Bacchus offered Midas his choice of a reward, whatever he might wish. He asked that whatever he might touch should be changed into gold. Bacchus consented, though sorry that he had not made a better choice. Midas went his way, rejoicing in his new-acquired power, which he hastened to put to the test. He could scarce believe his eyes when he found a twig of an oak, which he plucked from the branch, become gold in his hand. He took up a stone; it changed to gold. He touched a sod; it did the same. He took up an apple from the tree; you would have thought he had robbed the garden of the Hesperides. His joy knew no bounds, and as soon as he got home, he ordered the servants to set a splendid repast on the table. Then he found to his dismay that whether he touched bread, it hardened in his hand; or put a morsel to his lip, it defied his teeth. He took a glass of wine, but it flowed down his throat like melted gold.

In consternation at the unprecedented affliction, he strove to divest himself of his power; he hated the gift he had lately coveted. But all in vain; starvation seemed to await him. He raised his arms, all shining with gold, in prayer to Bacchus, begging to be delivered from his glittering destruction. Bacchus, merciful deity, heard and consented. 'Go,' said he, 'to River Pactolus, trace its fountain-head, there plunge yourself and body in, and wash away your fault and its punishment.' He did so, and scarce had he touched the waters before the gold-creating power passed into them, and the river sands became changed into gold, as they remain to this day.

From *The Age of Fable* by Thomas Bulfinch

 **acchus,** on a certain occasion, found his old schoolmaster and foster-father, Silenus, missing. The old man had been drinking, and in that state wandered away, and was found by some peasants, who carried him to their king, Midas. Midas recognized him, and treated him hospitably, entertaining him for ten days and nights with an unceasing round of jollity. On the eleventh day he brought Silenus back, and restored him in safety to his pupil. Whereupon Bacchus offered Midas his choice of a reward, whatever he might wish. He asked that what ever he might touch should be changed into gold. Bachus consented, though sorry that he had not made a better choice. Midas went his way, rejoicing in his new acquired power, which he hastened to put to the test. He could scarce believe his eyes when he found a twig of an oak, which he plucked from the branch, become gold in his hand. He took up a stone; it changed to gold. He touched a sod; it did the same. He took up an apple from the tree; you would have thought he had robbed the Garden of the Hesperides. His joy knew no bounds, and as soon as he got home, he ordered the servants to set a splendid repast on the table. Then he found to his dismay that whether he touched bread, it hardened in his hands; or put a morsel to his lips, it defied his teeth. He took a glass of wine, but it flowed down his throat like melted gold.

In consternation at the unprecedented affliction, he strove to divest himself of his power: he hated the gift he had lately coveted. But all in vain; starvation seemed to await him. He raised his arms, all shining with gold, in prayer to Bacchus, begging to be delivered from his glittering destruction. Bacchus, merciful deity, heard and consented. 'Go,' said he, 'to River Pactolus, trace its fountain head, there plunge yourself and body in, and wash away your fault and its punishment.' He did so, and scarce had he touched the waters before the gold-creating power passed into them, and the river sands became changed into gold, as they remain to this day.

From *The Age of Fable* By Thomas Bullfinch

THE HOUSE OF SECOND THOUGHTS

THE HOUSE OF SECOND THOUGHTS

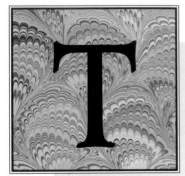

Thus, one and the same colour cannot be white and black. Nor can the same one action be good and bad: this law holds good with everything that is not substance. But one and the selfsame substance, while retaining its identity, is yet capable of admitting contrary qualities. The same individual person is at one time white, at another black, at one time warm, at another cold, at one time good, at another bad. This capacity is found nowhere else, though it might be maintained that a statement or opinion was an exception to the rule. The same statement, it is agreed, can be both true and false. For if the statement 'he is sitting' is true, yet, when the person in question has risen, the same statement will be false. The same applies to opinions. For if any one thinks truly that a person is sitting, yet, when that person has risen, this same opinion, if still held, will be false. Yet although this exception may be allowed, there is, nevertheless, a difference in the manner in which the thing takes place. It is by themselves changing that substances admit contrary qualities. It is thus that that which was hot becomes cold, for it has entered into a different state. Similarly that which was white becomes black, and that which was bad good, by a process of change; and in the same way in all other cases it is by changing that substances are capable of admitting contrary qualities. But statements and opinions themselves remain unaltered in all respects: it is by the alteration in the facts of the case that the contrary quality comes to be theirs. The statement 'he is sitting' remains unaltered, but it is at one time true, at another false, according to circumstances. What has been said of statements applies also to opinions. Thus, in respect of the manner in which the thing takes place, it is the peculiar mark of substance that it should be capable of admitting contrary qualities; for it is by itself changing that it does so.

If, then, a man should make this exception and contend that statements and opinions are capable of admitting contrary qualities, his contention is unsound. For statements and opinions are said to have this capacity, not because they themselves undergo modification, but because this modification occurs in the case of something else. The truth or falsity of a statement depends on facts, and not on any power on the part of the statement itself of admitting contrary qualities. In short, there is nothing which can alter the nature of statements and opinions. As, then, no change takes place in themselves, these cannot be said to be capable of admitting contrary qualities.

But it is by reason of the modification which takes place within the substance itself that a substance is said to be capable of admitting contrary qualities; for a substance admits within itself either disease or health, whiteness or blackness. It is in this sense that it is said to be capable of admitting contrary qualities.

From *Categories* by Aristotle

Thus, one and the same colour cannot be white and black. Nor can the same one action be good and bad: this law holds good with everything that is not substance. But one and the self-same substance, while retaining its identity, is yet capable of admitting contrary qualities. The same individual person is at one time white, at another black, at one time warm, at another cold, at one time good, at another bad. This capacity is found nowhere else, though it might be maintained that a statement or opinion was an exception to the rule. The same statement, it is agreed, can be both true and false. For if the statement "he is sitting" is true yet, when the person in question has risen, the same statement will be false. The same applies to opinions. For if any one thinks truly that a person is sitting, yet, when that person has risen, this same opinion, if still held, will be false. Yet although this exception may be allowed, there is, nevertheless, a difference in the manner in which the thing takes place. It is by themselves changing that substances admit contrary qualities. It is thus that that which was hot becomes cold, for it has entered into a different state. Similarly that which was white becomes black, and that which was bad, good, by a process of change; and in the same way in all other cases it is by changing that substances are capable of admitting contrary qualities. But statements and opinions themselves remain unaltered in all respects: it is by the alteration in the facts of the case that the contrary quality comes to be theirs. The statement 'he is sitting' remains unaltered, but it is at one time true, at another false, according to circumstances. What has been said of statements applies also to opinions. Thus, in respect of the manner in which the thing takes place, it is the peculiar mark of substance that it should be capable of admitting contrary qualities; for it is by itself changing that it does so.

If, then, a man should make this exception and contend that statements and opinions are capable of admitting contrary qualities, his contention is unsound. For statements and opinions are said to have this capacity, not because they themselves undergo modification, but because this modification occurs in the case of something else. The truth or falsity of a statement depends on facts, and not on any power on the part of the statement itself of admitting contrary qualities. In short, there is nothing which can alter the nature of statements and opinions. As, then, no change takes place in them selves, these cannot be said to be capable of admitting contrary qualities.

But it is by reason of the modification which takes place within the substance itself that a substance is said to be capable of admitting contrary qualities: for a substance admits within itself either disease or health, whiteness or blackness. It is in this sense that it is said to be capable of admitting contrary qualities.

from *Categories* by Aristotle

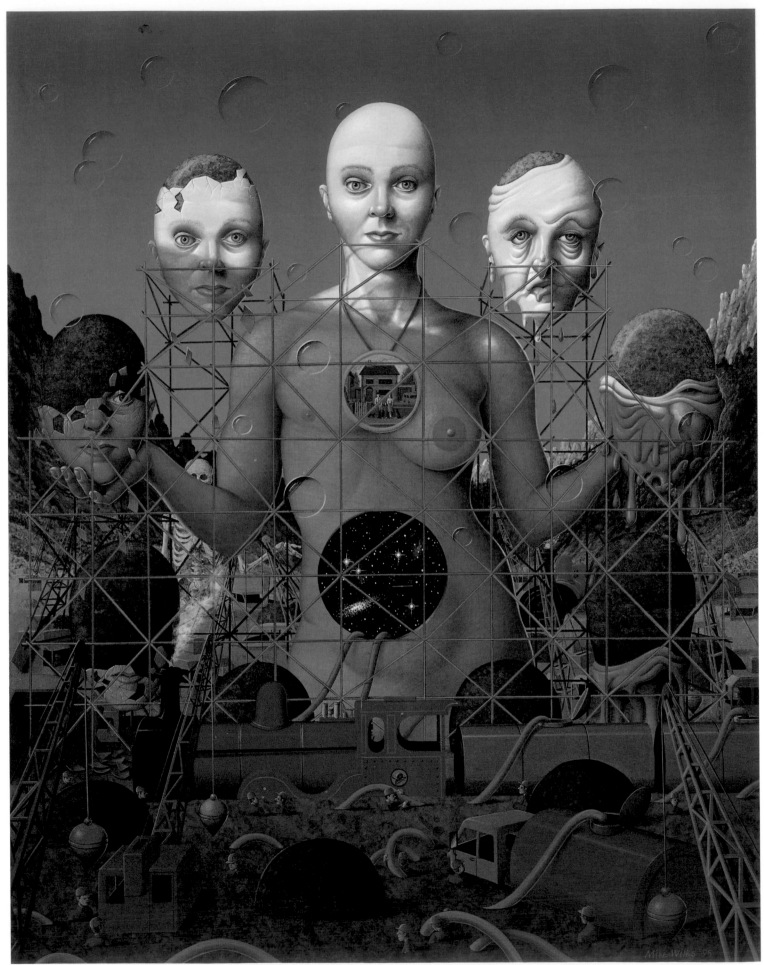

THE GRAVITY MINE

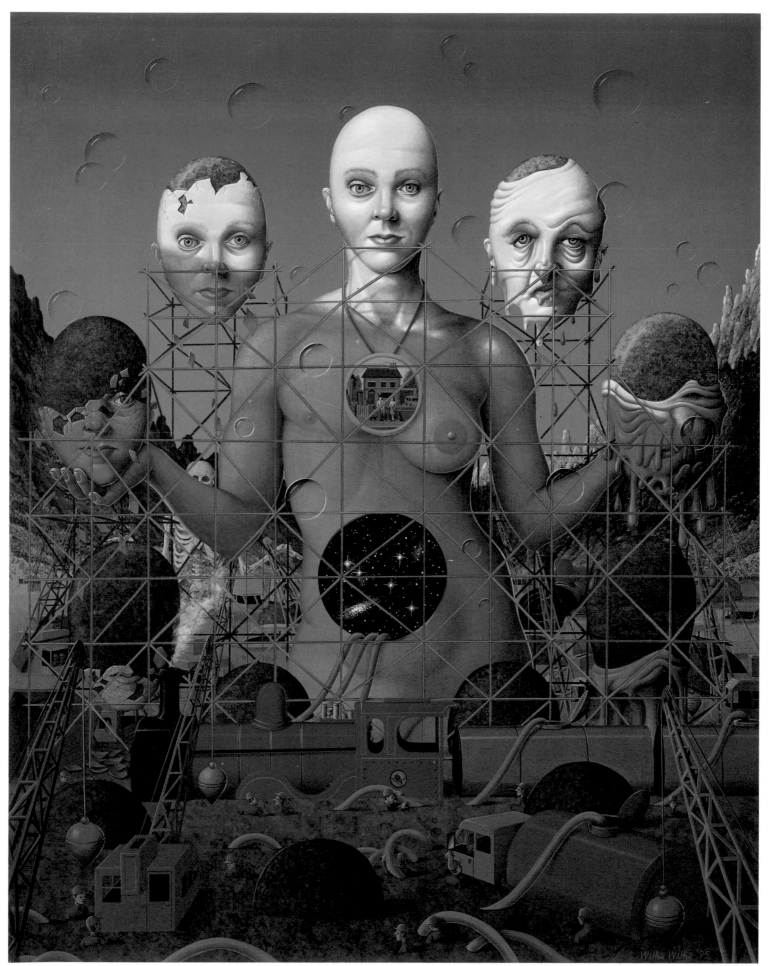

THE GRAVITY MINE

hen busie at my Book I was upon a certain Night,
This Vision here exprest appear'd unto my dimmed sight:
A Toad full Rudy I saw, did drink the juice of Grapes so fast,
Till over-charged with the broth, his Bowels all to brast:
And after that, from poyson'd Bulk he cast his Venom fell,
For Grief and Pain whereof his Members all began to swell;
With drops of Poysoned sweat approaching thus his secret Den,
His cave with blasts of fumous Air he all bewhited then:
And from the which in space a Golden Humour did ensue,
Whose falling drops from high did stain the soyl with ruddy hue.
And when his Corps the force of vital breath began to lack,
This dying Toad became forthwith like Coal for colour Black:
Thus drowned in his proper veins of poysoned flood;
For term of Eighty days and Four he rotting stood
By Tryal then his Venom to expel I did desire;
For which I did commit his Carkass to a gentle Fire:
Which done, a Wonder to the sight, but more to be rehearst;
The Toad with Colours rare through every side was pierc'd;
And White appear'd when all the sundry hews were past:
Which after being tincted Ruddy, for evermore did last.
Then of the Venom handled thus a Medicine I did make;
Which Venom kills, and saveth such a Venom chance to take:
Glory be to him the granter of such secret ways,
Dominium, and Honour both, with Worship, and with Praise.
Amen.

The Vision of Sir George Ripley, Cannon of Bridlington, Unfolded
(A fifteenth-century alchemical text)

hen busie at my book I was upon a certain Night,
This Vision here exprest appear'd unto my dimmed sight:
A Toad full Rudy I saw, did drink the juice of Grapes so fast,
Till over-charged with the broth, his Bowels all to brast:
And after that, from poyson'd Bulk he cast his Venom fell,
For Grief and Pain whereof his Members all began to swell;
With drops of Poysoned sweat approaching thus his secret Den,
His cave with blasts of fumous Air he all bewhited then:
And from the which in space a *G*olden Humour did ensue,
Whose falling drops from high did stain the soil with ruddy hue.
And when his Corps the force of vital breath began to lack,
This dying Toad became forthwith like Coal for colour Black.
Thus drowned in his proper veins of poysoned flood;
For term of Eighty days and Four he rottin' stood.
By Tryal then his Venom to expell l did desire;
For which I did commit his Carkass to a gentle Fire:
Which done, a Wonder to the sight, but more to be rehears't;
The Toad with Colours rare through every side was pierc'd;
And White appeared when all the Sundry hews were past:
Which after being tincted Ruddy, for evermore did last.
Then of the Venom handled thus a Medicine I did make;
Which Venom kills, and saveth such a Venom chance to take:
Glory be to Him the granter of such secret ways,
Dominium, and Honour both, with Worship, and with Praise.
*A*men.

The Vision of Sir George Ripley, Cannon of Bridlington, Unfolded
(A fifteenth-century Alchemical text)

THE INVENTION OF FARAWAY PLACES

THE INVENTION OF FARAWAY PLACES

'In the end I divided my well-armed crew into two parties with a leader for each. Of one party I myself took charge; the other I gave to the noble Eurylochus. Then we shook lots in a bronze helmet and out jumped the lot of the great-hearted Eurylochus, so he went off with his twenty-two men, a tearful company, leaving us, who stayed behind, weeping too. In a clearing in a glade they came upon Circe's house, built of polished stone. Prowling about the place were mountain wolves and lions that Circe had bewitched with her magic drugs. They did not attack my men, but rose on their hind legs to fawn on them, with much wagging of their long tails, like dogs fawning on their master as he comes from table for the tasty bits he always brings. In the same way these wolves and lions with great claws fawned round my men. Terrified at the sight of the formidable beasts, they stood in the palace porch of the goddess with the lovely tresses. They could hear Circe within, singing in her beautiful voice as she went to and fro at her great and everlasting loom, on which she was weaving one of those delicate, graceful and dazzling fabrics that goddesses make.

'Polites, an authoritative man and the one in my party whom I liked and trusted most, now took the lead. "Friends," he said, "there is someone in the castle working at a loom. The whole place echoes to that lovely voice. It's either a goddess or a woman. Let us call to her immediately."

'So they called and Circe came out at once, opened the polished doors, and invited them to enter. In their innocence, the whole party followed her in. But Eurylochus suspected a trap and stayed outside. Circe ushered the rest into her hall, gave them seats and chairs to sit on, and then prepared them a mixture of cheese, barley-meal, and yellow honey flavoured with Pramnian wine. But into this dish she introduced a noxious drug, to make them lose all memory of their native land. And when they had emptied the bowls which she had handed them, she drove them with blows of a stick into the pigsties. Now they had pig's heads and bristles, and they grunted like pigs; but their minds were as human as they had been before. So, weeping, they were penned in their sties. Then Circe flung them some forest nuts, acorns and cornel-berries - the usual food of pigs that wallow in the mud.'

From *The Odyssey* by Homer

'In the end I divided my well armed crew into two parties with a leader for each. Of one party I myself took charge, the other I gave to the noble Eurylochus. Then we shook lots in a bronze helmet and out jumped the lot of the great-hearted Eurylochus, so he went off with his twenty-two men, a tearful company, leaving us, who stayed behind, weeping too. In a clearing in a glade they came upon Sirces' house, built of polished stone. Prowling about the place were mountain wolves and lions that Circe had bewitched with her magic drugs. They did not attack my men, but rose on their hind legs to fawn on them, with much wagging of their long tails, like dogs fawning on their master as he comes from table for the tasty bites he always brings. In the same way these wolves and lions with great claws fawned round my men. Terrified at the sight of the formidable beasts, they stood in the palace porch of the goddess with the lovely tresses. They could hear Circle within, singing in her beautiful voice as she went to and fro at her great and everlasting loom, on which she was weaving one of those delicate, graceful and dazzling fabrics that goddesses make.

'Polites, an authoritative man and the one in my party whom I liked and trusted most, now took the lead. "Friends," he said, "there is someone in the castle working at a loom. The whole place echoes to that lovely voice. It's either a goddess or a woman. Let us call to her immediately.'

"So they called and Circe came out at once, opened the polished doors, and invited them to enter. In their innocence, the whole party followed her in. But Eurylochus suspected a trap and stayed outside. Circe ushered the rest into her hall, gave them seats and chairs to sit on, and then prepared them a mixture of cheese, barley-meal, and yellow honey-flavoured with Pramnian wine. But into this dish she introduced a noxious drug, to make them lose all memory of their native land. And when they had emptied the bowls which she had handed them, she drove them with blows of a stick, into the pigsties. Now they had pig's heads and bristles, and they grunted like pigs; but their minds' were as human as they had been before. So, weeping, they were penned in their sties. Then Circe flung them some forest nuts, acorns and cornell berries - the usual food of pigs that wallow in the mud.'

From *The Odyssey* by Homer

THE VIEW FROM LA ROQUE

THE VIEW FROM LE ROQUE

And then insensibly there came the strange change which I had noticed in the night. Her breathing grew stertorous, the mouth opened, and the pale gums, drawn back, made the teeth look longer and sharper than ever. In a sort of sleep-waking, vague, unconscious way she opened her eyes, which were now dull and hard at once, and said in a soft voluptuous voice, such as I had never heard from her lips:-

'Arthur! Oh, my love, I am glad you have come! Kiss me!' Arthur bent eagerly over to kiss her; but at that instant Van Helsing, who, like me, had been startled by her voice, swooped upon him, and catching him by the neck with both hands, dragged him back with a fury of strength which I never thought he could have possessed, and actually hurled him almost across the room.

'Not for your life!' he said; 'not for your living soul and hers!' And he stood between them like a lion at bay.

Arthur was so taken aback that he did not for a moment know what to do or say; and before any impulse of violence could seize him he realised the place and the occasion, and he stood silent, waiting.

I kept my eyes fixed on Lucy, as did Van Helsing, and we saw a spasm as of rage flit like a shadow over her face; the sharp teeth clamped together. Then her eyes closed, and she breathed heavily.

Very shortly after she opened her eyes in all their softness, and putting out her poor pale, thin hand, took Van Helsing's great brown one; drawing it to her, she kissed it. 'My true friend,' she said, in a faint voice, but with untellable pathos, 'my true friend, and his! Oh, guard him, and give him peace!'

'I swear it!' said he solemnly, kneeling beside her and holding up his hand, as one who registers an oath. Then he turned to Arthur, and said to him; 'Come, my child, take her hand in yours, and kiss her on the forehead, and only once.'

Their eyes met instead of their lips; and so they parted.

Lucy's eyes closed; and Van Helsing, who had been watching closely, took Arthur's arm, and drew him away.

And then Lucy's breathing became stertorous again, and all at once it ceased.

'It is all over,' said Van Helsing. 'She is dead!'

From *Dracula* by Bram Stoker

nd then insensibly there came the strange change which I had noticed in the night. Her breathing grew stertorous, the mouth opened, and the pale gums, drawn back, made the teeth look longer and sharper than ever. In a sort of sleep-waking, vague, unconscious way she opened her eyes, which were now dull and hard at once, and said in a soft, voluptuous voice, such as I had never heard from her lips:

'Arthur! Oh, my love, I am glad you have come! Kiss me!' Arthur bent eagerly over to kiss her: but at that instant Van Helsing, who, like me, had been startled by her voice, swooped upon him, and catching him by the neck with both hands, dragged him back with a fury of strength which I never thought he could have possessed, and actually hurled him almost across the room.

'Not for your life!' he said; ' not for your living soul and hers!' And he stood between them like a lion at bay.

Arthur was so taken aback that he did not for a moment know what to do or say; and before any impulse of violence could seize him he realised the place and the occasion, and he stood silent, waiting.

I kept my eyes fixed on Lucy, as did Van Helsing, and we saw a spasm as of rage flit like a shadow over her face; the sharp teeth clamped together. Then her eyes closed and she breathed heavily.

Very shortly after she opened her eyes in all their softness, and putting out her poor pale, thin hand, took Van Helsing's great brown one; drawing it to her, she kissed it. 'My true friend,' she said, in a faint voice, but with untellable pathos, 'my true friend, and his! Oh, guard him, and give him peace!'

'I swear it!' said he solemnly, kneeling beside her and holding up his hand, as one who registers an oath. Then he turned to Arthur, and said to him; "Come, my child, take her hand in yours, and kiss her on the forhead, and only once.'

Their eyes met instead of their lips; and so they parted.

Lucy's eyes closed; and Van Helsing, who had been watching closely, took Arthur's arm, and drew him away.

And then Lucy's breathing became stertorous again, and all at once it ceased.

'It is all over,' said Van Helsing: 'She is dead.'

From *Dracula* by Bram Stoker

THE CANNIBAL LUNCHEON CLUB

THE CANNIBAL LUNCHEON CLUB

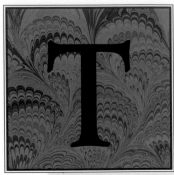

There was a cry heard, and a crash. The cry was so horrible in its agony that the frightened servants woke, and crept out of their rooms. Two gentlemen, who were passing in the Square below, stopped, and looked up at the great house. They walked on till they met a policeman, and brought him back. The man rang the bell several times, but there was no answer. Except for a light in one of the top windows, the house was all dark. After a time, he went away, and stood in the adjoining portico and watched.

'Whose house is that, constable?' asked the elder of the two gentlemen.

'Mr Dorian Gray's, sir,' answered the policeman.

They looked at each other, as they walked away, and sneered. One of them was Sir Henry Ashton's uncle.

Inside, in the servants' part of the house, the half-clad domestics were talking in low whispers to each other. Old Mrs Leaf was crying, and wringing her hands. Francis was as pale as death.

After about a quarter of an hour, he got the coachman and one of the footmen and crept upstairs. They knocked, but there was no reply. They called out. Everything was still. Finally, after vainly trying to force the door, they got on the roof, and dropped down onto the balcony. The windows yielded easily: their bolts were old.

When they entered, they found hanging upon the wall a splendid portrait of their master as they had last seen him, in all the wonder of his exquisite youth and beauty. Lying on the floor was a dead man, in evening dress, with a knife in his heart. He was withered, wrinkled, and loathsome of visage. It was not till they had examined his rings that they recognised who it was.

From *The Picture of Dorian Gray* by Oscar Wilde

here was a cry heard, and a crash. The cry was so horrible in its agony that the frightened servants awoke, and crept out of their rooms. Two gentlemen, who were passing in the Square below, stopped, and looked up at the great house. They walked on till they met a policeman, and brought him back. The man rang the bell several times, but there was no answer. Except for a light in one of the top windows, the house was all dark. After a time, he went away, and stood in the adjoining portico and watched.

'Whose house is that, Constable?' asked the elder of the two gentlemen.

'Mr Dorian Grey's, Sir,' answered the policeman.

They looked at each other, as they walked away, and sneered. One of them was Sir Henry Ashtons' uncle.

Inside, in the servant's part of the house, the half-clad domestics were talking in low whispers to each other. Old Mrs. Leaf was crying, and wringing her hands. Frances was as pale as death.

After about a quarter of an hour, he got the coachman and one of the footmen and crept upstairs. They knocked, but there was no reply. They called out. Everything was still. Finally, after vainly trying to force the door, they got on the roof, and dropped down onto the balcony. The windows yielded easily; their bolts were old.

When they entered, they found hanging upon the wall a splendid portrait of their master as they had last seen him, in all the wonder of his exquisite youth and beauty. Lying on the floor was a dead man in evening dress, with a knife in his heart. He was withered, wrinkled, and loathsome of visage. It was not till they had examined his rings that they recognized who it was.

From *The Picture of Dorian Grey* by Oscar Wild

LIGHT SLEEPER

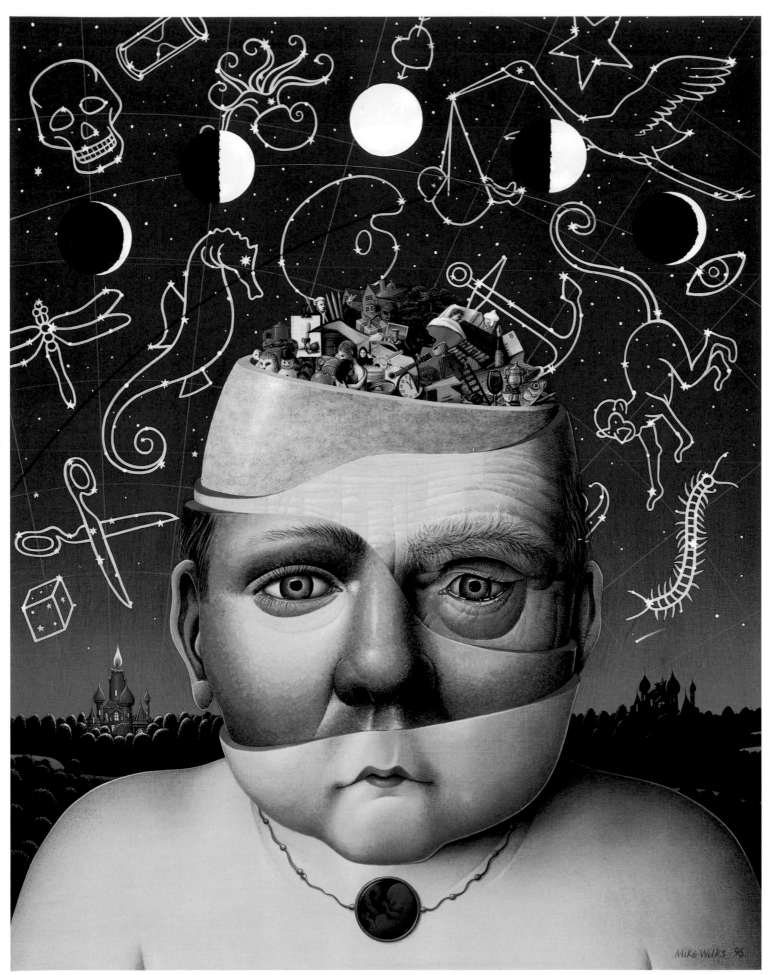

LIGHT SLEEPER

The Osiris the scribe Ani, whose word is truth, saith: I am the girdle of the garment of the god Nu, which giveth light, and shineth, and belongeth to his breast, the illuminer of the darkness, the uniter of the two Rehti deities, the dweller in my body, through the great spell of the words of my mouth. I rise up, but he who was coming after me hath fallen. He who was with him in the Valley of Abtu hath fallen. I rest. I remember him. The god Hu hath taken possession of me in my town. I found him there. I have carried away the darkness by my strength, I have filled the Eye [of Ra] when it was helpless, and when it came not on the festival of the fifteenth day. I have weighed Sut in the celestial houses against the Aged One who was with him. I have equipped Thoth in the House of the Moon-god, when the fifteenth day of the festival come not. I have taken possession of the Urrt Crown. Truth is in my body; turquoise and crystal are its months. My homestead is there among the lapis-lazuli, among the furrows thereof. I am Hem-Nu, the lightener of the darkness. I have come to lighten the darkness; it is light. I have lightened the darkness. I have overthrown the ashmiu-fiends. I have sung hymns to those who dwell in the darkness. I have made to stand up the weeping ones, whose faces were covered over; they were in a helpless state of misery. Look ye upon me. I am Hem-Nu. I will not let you hear concerning it. (I have fought. I am Hem-Nu. I have lightened the darkness. I have come. I have made an end to the darkness which hath become light indeed.)

(The Chapter of) Making the Transformation Into the God Who Lighteneth the Darkness
From *The Egyptian Book of the Dead*

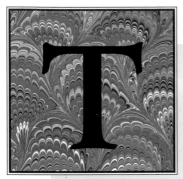

The Osiris the scribe Ani, whose word is truth, saith: I am the girdle of the garment of the god Nu, which giveth light, and shineth, and belongeth to his beast, the illuminer of the darkness, the united of the two Rehti deities, the dweller in my body, through the great spell of the words of my mouth. I rise up, but he who was coming after me hath fallen. He who was with him in the valley of Abtu hath fallen. I rest. I remember him. The God Hu hath taken possession of me in my town. I found him there. I have carried away the darkness by my strength, I have filled the Eye (of Ra) when it was helpless, and when it came not on the festival of the fifteenth day. I have weighted Sut in the celestial house against the Aged One who was with him. I have equipped Thoth in the House of the Moon-god, when the fifteenth day of the festival came not. I have taken possession of the Urtt Crown. Truth is in my body; turquoise and cristal are its months. My homestead is there among the lapis-lazulii, among the furrows thereof. I am Hem-Nu, the lightener of the darkness. I have come to lighten the darkness; it is light. I have lightened the darkness. I have overthrown the ashmiu-fiends. I have sung hymns to those who dwell in the darkness. I have made to stand up the weeping ones, whose faces were covered over; they were in a helpless state of misery. Look ye upon me. I am Hem-Nu. I will not let you hear concerning it. (I have fought. I am Hem-Nu. I have lightened the darkness. I have come. I have made an end to the darkness which hath become light indeed).

(The Chapter of) Making the Transformation Into the God Who Lighteneth the Darkness
From *The Egyptian Book of the Dead.*

THE GLOWING ASSASSINS TAKE PRIDE IN THEIR WORK

THE GLOWING ASSASSINS TAKE PRIDE IN THEIR WORK

All that which is to be found inside can be known thanks to the outside.

God did not wish it, that everything He gave to man for his own and for his profit should remain hidden... And if He has concealed certain things, He has give each one a mark visible from outside by means of particular signs - like a man who has buried some treasure and, in order to find it again, marks the spot.

We men discover all that a mountain hides thanks to exterior signs and through correspondences; and in the same way we find out all the properties of plants and what there is inside stones. There is nothing in the depths of the sea, nothing in the heights of the firmament, that man is not capable of discovering. No mountain is so vast as to conceal what it encloses from the eyes of man. Everything is revealed by signs... In the same way, all that a man encloses can be seen from the outside, and thus, by observing the exterior, we can get to know the inside...

From *Opus Paramirum*
by Philippus Aureolus Theophrastus Bombast Von Hohenheim, called Paracelsus the Great

All that which is to be found inside can be known thanks to the outside.

God did not wish it, that everything He gave to man for his own and for his profit should remain hidden... And if He has concealed certain things. He has give each one a mark visible from outside by means of particular signs - like a man who has buried some treasure and, in order to find it again, marks the spot.

We men discover all that a mountain hides thanks to exterior signs and through correspondences; and in the same way we find out all the properties of plants and what there is inside stones. There is nothing in the depths of the sea, nothing in the heights of the firmament, that man is not capable of discovering. No mountain is so vast as to conceal what it encloses from the eyes of man. Everything is revealed by signs... In the same way, all that a man encloses can be seen from the outside, and thus, by observing the exterior, we can get to know the inside....

From *Opus paramirum*
by Philippus Aureolus Theophrastus Bombast Von Hohenheim, called Paracelsus the Great

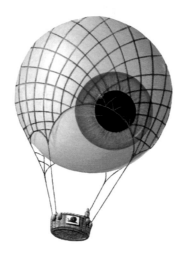

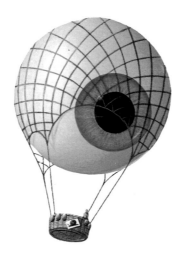

PENGUIN STUDIO

Published by the Penguin Group
Penguin Putnam Inc., 375 Hudson Street, New York, New York 10014, U.S.A.
Penguin Books Ltd, 27 Wrights Lane, London, W8 5TZ, England
Penguin Books Australia Ltd, Ringwood, Victoria, Australia
Penguin Books Canada Ltd, 10 Alcorn Avenue, Toronto, Ontario, Canada M4V 3B2
Penguin Books (NZ) Ltd, 182–190 Wairau Road, Auckland 10, New Zealand

Penguin Books Ltd, Registered Offices: Harmondsworth, Middlesex, England

First American edition
Published in 1997 by Penguin Studio, a member of Penguin Putnam Inc.

1 3 5 7 9 10 8 6 4 2

Copyright © Mike Wilks, 1997
All rights reserved.

Excerpt from *The Odyssey* by Homer, translated by
E. V. Rieu, revised translation by D. C. H. Rieu (Penguin Classics 1946,
revised translation 1991), copyright © 1946 by E. V. Rieu, this revised translation
copyright © the Estate of the late E. V. Rieu, and D. C. H. Rieu, 1991.
Reproduced by permission of Penguin Books Ltd.

CIP data available upon request

ISBN 0-670-87666-6

The moral right of the author has been asserted.

Printed in Italy by L.E.G.O., Vicenza
Color origination by Colorlito Rigogliosi, Milan